The Plant That Almost Ate the World

By Tisha Hamilton
Illustrated by Bruce Van Patter

Modern Curriculum Press
Parsippany, New Jersey

Cover and book design by Stephen Barth

Modern Curriculum Press
An imprint of Pearson Learning
299 Jefferson Road, P.O. Box 480
Parsippany, NJ 07054–0480

www.pearsonlearning.com

1-800-321-3106

ISBN 0-7652-2166-7

2 3 4 5 6 7 8 9 10 11   MA   07 06 05 04 03 02 01

Contents

For Will, who is wild in all the best ways!

Chapter 1

Mrs. Greenspan's Problem

As Mrs. Greenspan got ready for school, she couldn't help worrying a little bit. Janie Ferguson was in her class. Janie Ferguson was a good student. She also had a lot of enthusiasm. Mrs. Greenspan thought enthusiasm was a good thing, but Janie's enthusiasm usually went too far.

As she worked, Mrs. Greenspan remembered some of the overly enthusiastic things Janie had done. When the class had made model volcanoes for a science project, Janie had decided that if a little baking soda made her volcano erupt, a lot of baking soda would be even better. She'd poured in box after box, and the volcano had burped and fizzled and overflowed for a long, long time.

The class had stood on their desks as the foam flowed out the door and down the hall. When the foam reached the principal's office, she had called the fire department. The firefighters didn't know what else to do, so they tried to wash the foam away with water. That just made it worse. School was dismissed early that day.

It had been days before the last of the foam finally dried up and blew away. Even now, Mrs. Greenspan often thought she heard little burbles in odd places when it rained.

On Pet Day, Janie had brought a goat, four dogs, six cats, and seven white mice. School was dismissed early that day too, as everyone was busy keeping the mice away from the cats, the cats away from the dogs, and the goat away from the books.

Now it was time to remind everyone about the One Hundredth Day Celebration. The students and the teachers all loved this day because there were parties in the classrooms, exhibits in the halls, and a musical program on the school stage.

Every year Mrs. Greenspan did something special with her class for the One Hundredth Day Celebration. She always asked them to make a collection of 100 things. What the things would be was up to each student, but they had to start collecting now so they had time to get their collection ready. That's why Mrs. Greenspan wanted to make sure she reminded them about it.

At least one student always brought in 100 pennies. Other favorites were rocks, shells, and toy cars. Sometimes she got 100 key chains, baseball cards, paper clips, and erasers. One year she even got 100 toothbrushes.

The collections always turned out to be the most fun project in every school year. This year was different, though. What would Janie do?

In Janie's class last year, her teacher had asked the students to do activities that added up to 100. One student had done 100 hops. Another had written his name 100 times. Another had done 100 spins and had to go to the nurse.

Janie had gotten 100 friends to make a huge, human pyramid. Then Janie had climbed up to the top. The problem had been getting everyone down without anyone falling. That had been a big problem, Mrs. Greenspan remembered.

Now Mrs. Greenspan took a deep breath as her students came into the classroom. "Good morning," she told her students, smiling.

Her students all smiled back as she went on. "As you know, we'll be having a One Hundredth Day Celebration again this year," she said. The class cheered. They all loved the One Hundredth Day Celebration.

"In my class we always do collections of 100 things," Mrs. Greenspan continued. "You'll need to start soon in order to have 100 by the time we celebrate 100 days of school. What you collect is up to you, but since we're studying earth science this year, let's try to come up with nature collections. For tonight's homework, write a paragraph explaining what your collection will be and why."

Mrs. Greenspan saw that Janie's eyes were bright with excitement. "Oh, no," she thought.

Chapter 2

Janie's Problem

Janie walked home as usual that afternoon with her friends Marcella and Sean. She was excited about the idea of making a collection, but she couldn't think of anything to collect. Marcella had already decided to make a leaf collection, so Janie couldn't do that. Sean had decided to collect rocks, so Janie couldn't do that either.

She thought about the cool stuff she'd collected on the beach this past summer. She had clam shells and snail shells, mussel shells and fan shells. She even had a real starfish.

Just as she was about to open her mouth to tell her friends what her project was going to be, Sean spoke up. "Did you see that huge pink shell Nina has? She spent the summer in Puerto Rico with her grandfather, and she found all kinds of really cool shells."

Janie's heart sank low and then lower as Sean added, "That's Nina's project." Oh well, Janie thought, my friends have all seen my shells anyway. I want to do something new.

Since she lived the closest to school, Janie's house was first on the way home. They turned down Forest Street and when they came to number 12, Janie stopped. She said goodbye to her friends and went inside.

"Uh-oh," Mrs. Ferguson said, looking up as Janie dumped her backpack in the kitchen.

"What's wrong?" Janie asked.

"I don't know," her mother answered. "Why don't you tell me? I said uh-oh when I saw that look on your face. Is something bothering you?"

Janie sighed. "I need to come up with an idea for a nature collection," she explained. "I was just talking to Sean and Marcella about what they're going to do. It seems as though every time I have an idea, it already belongs to someone else."

Janie's mother handed her an apple and poured her a glass of milk. "Maybe a snack will help you get your brain in gear," she said. "When you're finished, why don't you take a walk outside?" she added. "Maybe if you look around, something will come to you."

"Thanks, Mom," Janie said. The apple was crisp and sort of sweet and sour, just the way Janie liked it. The milk was ice-cold. She felt better already. She thought her mom was probably right about going outside, too.

Janie's mom went upstairs to the room she used as an office. She ran a mail-order business out of their home. Most of her orders came from her Internet Web site called The Bee's Knees. She sold all kinds of things with bee designs. Janie couldn't believe how many people collected this funny-looking stuff.

Janie sat, eating her apple and thinking about bees. Then she looked out the window next to the kitchen table. She could see her next-door neighbor, Mr. Mercato, working in his garden.

Mr. Mercato was moving from plant to plant. Janie watched for a while but couldn't figure out what he was doing. It looked as if he was tickling the flowers. Then it looked as if he was shaking them. Every so often he leaned down and did something Janie couldn't see.

Janie tossed her apple core in the garbage and drank the last of her milk. She put her empty glass in the sink and headed outside. She wanted to know what Mr. Mercato was doing.

Chapter 3

The Seed of an Idea

"Hi, Mr. Mercato," Janie called. She went around the prickly hedge that separated her backyard from Mr. Mercato's yard.

"Hello, Janie," Mr. Mercato said in his quiet way. Janie could see a large basket on the ground by his feet. The basket was full of dozens of little plastic bags. Each bag had been written on with black marker.

"What are you doing?" Janie asked.

"I'm collecting seeds," he told her.

Suddenly, it felt as if a big lightbulb had gone on inside Janie's head. "You collect seeds?" she asked, her eyes wide.

Mr. Mercato chuckled. "I collect seeds so I can plant them in the spring," he explained. Now Janie could see that when it looked as if Mr. Mercato was tickling or shaking the flowers, he was really jiggling them lightly. A small sprinkling of seeds would then fall out into his cupped hand, which he held under the flower.

18

Some seeds were small and round. Some were long and thin. Some were pale and some were dark. Janie found this all very interesting. "Can I help?" she asked.

"Well," Mr. Mercato said, "I'll let you try shaking one flower. You must be very careful."

Janie held a flower lightly in one hand and jiggled it up and down. The seeds came out faster than she thought they would. They would have fallen on the ground if Mr. Mercato hadn't quickly held his hand under Janie's.

"Do you see what I mean?" he asked. "You must be careful."

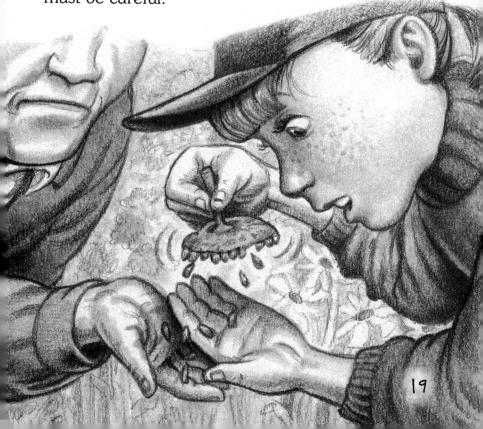

Janie tried another flower. This time she caught all of the seeds. Mr. Mercato talked as they went from flower to flower. At the end of a plant's growing season, he said, it started producing seeds. Sometimes the seeds were inside the flower and sometimes they were in little pods that came out of the stems.

When they got to the end of a row, Janie told Mr. Mercato about the collection Mrs. Greenspan had assigned. "I think a seed collection would be great. Could I have some of these seeds to start a seed collection?" she asked. "Please?" she added.

Mr. Mercato didn't say anything for a few moments. "Yes," he finally said. "You can have one of each kind, but not that one," he added, as Janie pinched a fat green seed pod off a tall, spiky plant.

"Why not?" Janie asked. "Isn't it a seed?"

"It is a seed, but the plant you took it from is a weed," said Mr. Mercato. "I spend too much time pulling weeds out of my garden as it is. I'm certainly not going to save weed seeds to plant next spring."

"It is interesting looking, though," Janie pointed out. "I'll keep it for my collection." She put it in her pocket.

"Every plant there is, including trees and flowers and weeds, produces seeds," Mr. Mercato said, "so you could look for different kinds of seeds everywhere you go." Then he showed Janie how to find grass seed, and even how to pop open a pea pod to get the seeds inside.

When Janie went home, she had 11 different kinds of seeds, including the weed seed. She showed them to her mom and told her about her idea for a collection.

"It's a great idea, and very unusual, too," said Mrs. Ferguson. "Tomorrow after school we'll go to the park by the river and hunt for seeds."

The river park would be a great place. There were lots of wildflowers and strange weedy plants that grew near the water. "Thanks, Mom," Janie said. "I can't wait!"

Chapter 4

Collecting Fever

The next day, Janie was nearly late for school because she kept stopping to collect seeds from any interesting plants she saw on the way. At lunchtime she carefully saved the seeds from her apple. She even asked Marcella for a piece of her orange so she could save the seeds from that. It seemed all Janie could think about were seeds.

In class the word *seed* kept finding its way into all of Janie's answers. Instead of saying 1776 when Mrs. Greenspan asked when the Declaration of Independence was signed, Janie answered, "Seventeen seventy seeds!" Janie had gone seed crazy.

The good thing was that Mrs. Greenspan had approved Janie's seed collection idea. Now no one else could use that idea. Mrs. Greenspan was happy, too, because she thought Janie's idea was harmless. Seeds were small. They didn't do anything at all, at least not until they were planted. Mrs. Greenspan couldn't imagine how seeds could be a problem. She sighed with relief.

24

After school Janie ran nearly all the way home. She couldn't wait to go to the park with her mother. When she got home, Janie emptied her backpack. Then she put some plain white envelopes and a black marker inside. She was ready to start collecting.

First she needed a snack, though. She chose a pear from the bowl on the table. She didn't have any pear seeds yet.

Janie's mother laughed. "Maybe you have enough seeds already," she said. "Maybe we don't have to visit the river park after all."

"Mom!" Janie cried. "I'm nowhere near having 100 seeds."

"Just kidding," her mother said, ruffling Janie's hair. "Let's go."

Once they were at the park, Janie saw all kinds
of plants. She rushed from plant to plant and
managed to get seeds from nearly all of them.
There were even acorns from the oak trees and
chestnuts from the chestnut trees.

Janie was so excited about finding seeds that
she began to go faster and faster. Her plan had
been to keep careful track of all the seeds she got
and to label them the way Mr. Mercato had
taught her. She forgot about her plan as she
gathered seeds and stuffed them in envelopes.
She figured she could always label the seeds
when she got home.

26

As she hurriedly stuffed the seeds in her backpack, she wasn't careful to close the envelopes. Now the seeds were starting to mix together inside her backpack.

Her seed gathering led her down to the river. While she was still looking around, she heard her mother calling, "Janie, it's time to go." Janie didn't stop. "JANIE," her mother yelled.

"All right, Mom," Janie finally answered. "I'll be right there."

She was about to go back up the hill when she spotted it. Growing out of a crack in a big rock was the strangest plant she had ever seen.

The plant had purple instead of green leaves. A big furry-looking seed pod was growing out of the top of the plant. Janie just knew there was a really interesting seed inside that pod.

"I've got to get that seed," she said to herself. She took off her backpack and started to scramble up the rock. She slipped back a few times, but finally she reached the plant. She shook the seed pod. Nothing happened. She shook it harder. It wouldn't open. Then she tugged and tugged at it.

She was about to give up when the pod opened with a loud pop! Janie's hat flew off as she fell backward. She saw a big hairy-looking seed fly out of the pod. It bounced down the rock and landed next to her backpack.

Janie scrambled back down the rock and picked up the strange seed. It felt sticky, so she quickly put it into her backpack and rubbed her hand on her jeans. She found her hat and put it back on. Then she ran to join her mom, who was waiting in the car.

As they drove home, Mrs. Ferguson looked over at Janie, who was holding her backpack on her lap. "You've got a lot of seeds in there," she said. "It looks like more than 100," she added.

Janie looked down. Her backpack was bulging with seeds. "I'll just have to pick out the best ones for my collection," Janie replied.

Janie ran up to her room as soon as she got home. She dumped the backpack onto her desk. Seeds tumbled out. Some bounced onto the floor and rolled into corners.

Janie started separating the seeds and making labels for the ones she could identify. Acorns and chestnuts were easy. Others were not.

Janie did the best she could, writing labels such as "pink flower" or "tall river plant" when she wasn't sure what the plant was called. Then she came to something really strange.

It was the big, fuzzy, sticky seed she had gotten from the plant in the rock, or that's what it *had* been. Now it was a big sticky seed ball. All kinds of seeds, small and large, were stuck to it.

Janie tried to get the seeds off, but the sticky stuff had hardened like cement. Janie tossed the seedy ball onto her windowsill. She'd try to unstick it all later.

Chapter 5

Janie's Experiment

Janie spent almost an hour in her room, happily sorting her seeds and making labels. This was going to be the best collection ever!

"JANIE!!" her mother yelled from downstairs. "It's dinnertime!"

Janie ran downstairs. She quickly took her seat next to her brother, Jim. He had just finished feeding all of his pets. The dogs, mice, cats, and goat that Janie had brought to school on Pet Day all belonged to him.

While they ate, the Fergusons told each other what they'd done that day. Mr. Ferguson had found three new springs for his collection. He was famous in the neighborhood for having just the right spring to fix something. "Someone gave me two old watch springs and one of those tiny springs you find in ballpoint pens," he said.

Jim talked about his pets. Several of his white mice now had babies. "I've got 60 white mice," he said proudly. "I just counted them."

Mrs. Ferguson talked about The Bee's Knees. "I got several orders today for bee plates," she said, "and someone asked about a beehive cookie jar."

Janie told everyone about her seed collection. Jim didn't think it was nearly as interesting as his pets. "Seeds don't do very much," he said.

After dinner, Janie brought all the dishes over to the sink. A yucky-looking pan of greasy water sat in the bottom of the sink.

"What's this?" Janie asked.

"I'm soaking the pan," Mr. Ferguson explained. "That way it's easier to clean."

"Why?" Janie wanted to know.

"Because when you soak it, it helps loosen all the sticky bits," her dad said. "See?" He dumped out the dirty water and began washing the pan. Janie could see how easily all the gooey bits of food came off. It gave her an idea.

When Janie and her dad had finished cleaning
up the kitchen, Janie went back upstairs to her
room. She had explained her new idea to her
dad. He thought it was a great idea, so he had
washed out an empty tin can for her to use.

Janie filled the can with warm water from the
sink in the bathroom. Then she carefully lowered
the sticky seed pod into the water. She figured
that if she soaked the sticky pod, the seeds that
were stuck to it would loosen in the same way
that soaking had worked on the pan. She put the
can on the corner of her desk, just under her
desk lamp. Then she did her homework.

After an hour Janie was finished. She checked the sticky seed ball by wiggling her fingers in the can. The seeds didn't seem to have loosened up at all, so Janie left the seed ball in the can.

When it was time for bed, Janie realized she was very tired. She put on her pajamas, brushed her teeth, and got into bed.

Just as she was falling asleep, Janie remembered the seed ball. "Oh well," she yawned, "I'll check it in the morning."

The next thing she knew, her mother was calling to her, "Janie! JANIE!! You're going to be late!" Janie had overslept!

She jumped out of bed. When her feet hit the floor, she was already running. The bathroom door slammed. Water gurgled. Janie's toothbrush swished. She was in such a hurry she forgot to check on the big seed ball.

It was a beautiful day, warm and sunny even though it was early autumn. Right before she left to shop for more bee items for The Bee's Knees, Mrs. Ferguson opened all the bedroom windows upstairs.

"This house needs some fresh air," she said. She didn't notice that something seemed to be growing in the can on Janie's desk.

As the sunlight poured through Janie's window, the can began to rock slightly. Small green shoots began to creep out of the top of the can. They moved slowly toward the sun.

Later that afternoon, before Janie came home from school, the wind picked up. It blew through Janie's bedroom window and scattered some of the seeds she had left lying around. A few small wispy seeds blew into the can, which by now had sprouted some vines.

Now the breeze began to rock a small paint jar that sat on the shelf above the can. The lid was loose because Janie had not tightened it the last time she had used the paint. The jar rocked and rocked, then suddenly tipped. The lid bounced off, and thick blue paint dripped into the can.

The vines burst up out of the can and reached outside the window. They poked through the screen and chased after the sunshine.

It was hard to say what caused this sudden explosion. Maybe it was the combination of the sticky seeds, the water, the sunshine, and the paint. Whatever it was, when the Fergusons got home later that day, they were in for a VERY big surprise.

Chapter 6

The Monster Plant

Mrs. Ferguson was having a great day. She had found all kinds of great bee things for The Bee's Knees. As she stuffed the things in her car, she looked at her watch. It was only 2:30 P.M. She still had plenty of time to drive by the school, pick up Janie and Jim, and get them to their 3:30 dentist appointments.

The dentist appointments took a long time. When they were finished, it was five o'clock, almost time for Mr. Ferguson's train to arrive. Usually he walked home from the train station, but today his family decided to surprise him by picking him up. Mrs. Ferguson drove straight from the dentist to the train station.

When Mr. Ferguson stepped off the train, it was 5:30 P.M. Because it was near dinnertime, the family decided to go out for pizza. So they drove straight from the train station to the best pizza place in town. They didn't go home first.

By now the strange plant in Janie's room had been growing for nearly nine hours. Some of the vines had grown out the window. Other vines had explored Janie's room. Then they had trailed out the door and down the hall to Jim's room.

In Jim's room the white mice began to squeak when they saw the vine crawling across the floor. They had never seen a plant move before, and they didn't like it.

When the vine reached the first cage, it wrapped itself around the door and pulled. The cage door opened. The mice leaped out quickly, trying to escape from the plant.

The vine that had grown out of Janie's window trailed down the side of the house. It reached toward one of the doghouses, then moved across the back steps. There it found something wonderful. Mr. Ferguson had left an open bag of lawn fertilizer on the steps. At 5:45 P.M. long green tendrils of plant were poking into the bag.

Mrs. Ferguson kept a compost pile in the backyard. She dumped banana peels, eggshells, old lettuce, and carrot peelings on it nearly every week. Every so often she stirred it all up by turning it over with a big shovel. After a while all this organic matter turned into a kind of black dirt that Mrs. Ferguson put around her roses every spring. She claimed it really helped her roses grow big and bushy.

By 6:15 the plant had covered the bag of fertilizer and the compost pile. Now it began to grow even faster as it spread across the lawn. Soon it was climbing the fence.

At 6:30 P.M. Mr. Mercato heard a loud barking coming from next door. "What's wrong with Jim Ferguson's dogs?" he said. He decided to take a look. He opened the back door.

Mr. Mercato's garden was no longer there. He stared in amazement at the enormous plant that now covered his backyard. When he looked in the direction the plant was coming from, he got an even bigger shock.

The place where the Fergusons' house had been was now a gigantic plant. If he looked carefully, Mr. Mercato could see part of the doors and windows underneath the plant. The wild barking was coming from the backyard.

"Don't worry!" he yelled toward the Fergusons' house. "I'll save you!" He ran back inside and dialed 911.

At 6:45 a fire truck pulled up in front of the Fergusons' house with its siren blaring. It was followed by two police cars and an ambulance. The firefighters jumped out of the truck and hooked up their hoses. They were going to try to blast the plant away from the house with water.

By now a crowd had gathered. The police tried
to keep them back. Finally, even the police had
to move back because the vines kept wrapping
around their ankles as they stood on the
Fergusons' lawn.

45

One of the neighbors yelled, "Where are the Fergusons? Are they all right?"

One of the police officers answered, "We haven't seen them. They must be trapped in the house." The crowd gasped.

Chapter 7

The Plant Goes to Town

Meanwhile, on the other side of town, the Fergusons finally decided they'd had enough pizza and it was time to go home. They piled into their car and drove toward Forest Street. When they were a block away, they saw a barricade up ahead. A police officer held up his hand to tell them to stop. It was 7 P.M.

Mrs. Ferguson rolled down the driver's side window. "Officer, can you tell me what's going on?" she asked.

"We have an important rescue going on," the police officer told them. "We have a report of a family trapped by a giant plant. I'm afraid I can't let you folks through. It's too dangerous."

The Fergusons all looked at each other. Who could it be, they wondered. Janie began to get a bad feeling about what was happening.

Mr. Ferguson leaned over to speak out the window. "Why, Officer, this is terrible," he said. "We live on this street, too, so it must be one of our neighbors."

The police officer looked down at a pad he was holding. "Yes, it's terrible," he agreed. "There's a whole family trapped at number 12 Forest Street. We've been trying to get them out for an hour, but that giant plant won't budge."

"That's funny," said Mrs. Ferguson in a wavering voice. "I thought I heard you say number 12 Forest Street."

"Yes, ma'am, you did," said the officer. "A family by the name of Ferguson is trapped at number 12 Forest Street."

Mrs. Ferguson leaped out of the car. "We live at number 12!" she shouted.

"We are the Ferguson family!" Mr. Ferguson yelled at the same time as he leaped out of his side of the car. Then Mr. Ferguson fainted.

The police officer quickly called an ambulance.
An emergency medical technician dashed up to
the Fergusons' car. He bent down and waved a
bottle of smelling salts under Mr. Ferguson's
nose. Mr. Ferguson opened his eyes.

As soon as Mr. Ferguson was able to get up,
everyone began talking at once.

"Can you tell us what kind of plant it is?" the
police officer wanted to know.

"Are you feeling better now?" asked the
emergency medical technician.

"Are you sure it's our house?" Mr. Ferguson
kept saying.

Just then the news reporters arrived. "Please, everyone be quiet," shouted a reporter with a microphone. "We can't record the sound if everyone's talking at once!"

Just as everyone stopped talking, a very small voice was heard. It was Janie.

"Um, what exactly does this plant look like?" she asked.

"Janie!" Mrs. Ferguson exclaimed. "Do you know anything about this?"

"Well," Janie began, "do you remember my seed collection and that weird sticky seed I found by the river?"

Now it was Mrs. Ferguson who looked as if she might faint. Mr. Ferguson patted her arm.

The police officer said something into his radio. Another police car raced up. The Fergusons got in. The first police officer moved the barricade just enough to let them through.

As the police car approached the Fergusons' house, it slowed down. The Fergusons stared in amazement. The street was covered with water, and their house was covered with an enormous plant. The firefighters had tried using the strong blast from the fire hose to push the plant away from the house. It had only made the plant grow bigger and thicker.

The vine was now beginning to move down the street, waving its leaves in the air. The neighbors who had been crowding in front of the house to get a better look began to back away.

Suddenly, one of the firefighters yelled, "Look at that!" Everyone turned.

In a second-floor window of the Ferguson house, something white was moving. Then it seemed to pour down the plant. Janie couldn't figure out what it was. Then she knew. It wasn't a white thing. Jim's 60 mice were escaping from the house together.

Dozens of white mice raced down the plant's thick stem. Around the side of the house came the goat, the dogs, and the cats. The goat had chewed through part of the plant and set all of the pets free. Everyone stared as the animals ran down the street.

The crowd of people began to panic. "If someone doesn't stop this thing," a woman yelled, "it will take over the whole town." Some of the neighbors ran toward their own homes to gather up their belongings. They were afraid their own homes were next.

Chapter 8

Who'll Save the Day?

Some of the firefighters moved toward the Ferguson house. Now they tried to chop the plant away from the house with their axes. The stems were too tough, though, and the axes kept bouncing off.

Finally the fire chief shouted, "All right, everyone, put down your axes." He said, "A team of scientists is on the way. Clear the area."

Soon the thunka-thunka-thunka sound of a helicopter could be heard getting closer and closer. It landed on the street in front of the Fergusons' house. Two women and a man, all wearing white lab coats, jumped out. They carefully stepped over the vine as it began curling around the helicopter.

The scientists' names were Dr. Green, Dr. Bean, and Dr. Sleeves. They immediately began taking all kinds of measurements. It was now exactly 7:30 P.M.

"The air temperature is 65 degrees Fahrenheit," said Dr. Green, looking at a small device in her hand. "Humidity is 78 percent."

"The diameter of the stem is approximately five feet," said Dr. Bean, holding a tape measure.

"The molecular structure of the plant shows a plant of aquatic nature," said Dr. Sleeves, as she examined a leaf under her microscope.

Meanwhile, a special team of police officers had been climbing all over the plant using ropes and pulleys. They were following the tangled stems and vines trying to figure out where the plant was coming from.

Suddenly the police chief's radio crackled. "They found it," the chief shouted. "It's a small window on the right-hand side of the back of the house. It has red-striped curtains," he added.

Janie groaned. The plant was coming from her room for sure.

Now the three scientists began asking Janie questions. They wanted to know everything she could tell them about the mysterious plant.

Janie described the place where she had found it. Then she explained how a bunch of seeds had gotten stuck to the big seed. Finally she told them about leaving it in a can of water.

"What kind of can was it?" Dr. Green wanted to know.

"It was an empty tomato sauce can," Mr. Ferguson told them. "I rinsed it out with water first. What does that have to do with anything?"

Dr. Bean made some notes on his pad.

"What about other conditions in the room?" Dr. Sleeves asked.

"Well, it was a beautiful day," said Mrs. Ferguson, "so the windows were open." Dr. Bean wrote this down, too.

The scientists put their heads together and began murmuring. They looked very serious. Then Dr. Green spoke up.

"We can't be absolutely sure," she said, "but we believe a combination of things created this monster plant. Perhaps the sticky substance on the big seed caused some of the seeds to mutate, or change into something else."

"Then perhaps some leftover tomato sauce in the can added a vital nutrient," Dr. Bean added.

"The water and the sun provided extra growing power," Dr. Sleeves concluded. "You don't mind if we take pictures, do you?"

"N-no," Mrs. Ferguson said slowly, "but who's going to get this plant out of here?"

"We were only hired to examine it, ma'am," said Dr. Green sternly. "We are scientists, not exterminators."

"We've tried everything," the fire chief said to Mr. Ferguson. "Nothing works."

"Help me!" cried a voice nearby. "Get me out of here and I'll take care of that plant!" It was Mr. Mercato. He'd been watching and listening to everything from an upstairs window. The vines had covered all the doors to his house, so he couldn't get out.

The firefighters quickly got a ladder so that Mr. Mercato could climb down. Soon he was telling everyone what to do. Janie was very relieved. Mr. Mercato knew everything about plants. She ran up to him and offered to help.

"OK, see if you can get the National Guard on the phone," Mr. Mercato directed the police chief. "We're going to need a lot of help."

Next he said something to Janie. She ran up to the fire chief. He scratched his head when he heard what she was asking him to do. "We'll do our best," he promised her.

Finally Mr. Mercato telephoned his friend Mr. Getzoff. He owned a factory that made waterproof fabric for raincoats.

At 8:30 P.M. the National Guard arrived. Mr. Getzoff pulled up in a truck from his factory at 8:45. By nine o'clock the fire chief had figured out how to change the hoses. Now instead of shooting water, they sucked it back up.

The National Guard got to work pulling long rolls of fabric from Mr. Getzoff's truck. It took them all night long, but by daybreak every inch of the plant was covered with the dark raincoat material.

Meanwhile, neither the Fergusons nor Mr. Mercato could get into their houses. They helped until they were too tired to do any more. Then they all went to a nearby motel and slept straight through until the next day.

The next day, school was canceled and businesses were closed because of the plant emergency. Later, everyone in town helped unwrap the plant, including Mrs. Greenspan. They gasped when the raincoat material came off. The stems that had been so thick and tough the day before were now skinny and limp.

Mr. Mercato looked down at the mess and smiled. "I'm no scientist, but I am a gardener," he said. "A plant needs water and sunshine in order to grow, and the surest way to make it stop growing is to keep it dry and dark."

After that it was easy to pull the plant away from the two houses. Fourteen garbage trucks came and hauled pieces away. The dogs, the cats, and the goat all came back once the plant was gone. The mice were never seen again.

After the last of the plant was gone, Mr. Mercato walked back to his house. The mayor of the town wanted to give him an award and a special dinner, but he politely said, "No, thank you. I have to get back to my garden." As far as he was concerned, that was that.

When it was finally time for the Hundredth Day Celebration, Mrs. Greenspan's class showed off their collections. Janie shared her seed collection, keeping each seed separate and dry.

People in town still talk about how Janie Ferguson's plant almost ate the world and how Mr. Mercato saved the day. Mrs. Greenspan still has her classes do collections for the Hundredth Day Celebration, but no seeds are allowed.

Glossary

ambulance   [AM byuh luns] a special automobile for carrying sick or injured people

aquatic   [uh KWAH tihk] growing or living in or upon water

barricade   [BAR uh kayd] anything that blocks the way

compost   [KAHM pohst] a mixture of decaying vegetables and other organic materials used to enrich soil

enthusiasm   [en THOO zee az um] a strong liking or interest

exterminators   [eks TUR mun ay turz] people whose work is getting rid of pests, such as rats and insects

fertilizer   [FUR tul eye zur] a chemical or organic substance put in the soil as food for plants

mutate   [MYOO tayt] to change in form

organic   [or GAN ihk] coming from living matter

panic   [PAN ihk] to have a sudden wild fear that is not controlled and can spread quickly